CARMEN NASR

Carmen Nasr is a British-Lebanese writer. Her play *The Climbers* will premiere in June 2022 at Theatre by the Lake, directed by Guy Jones. In 2017 Carmen won the Channel 4 Playwright's scheme with *Dubailand* and was awarded a year-long residency at the Finborough Theatre. Her first play *The House of My Father* was long-listed for the Bruntwood Prize for Playwriting in 2015. In February 2017 *Dubailand* premiered at the Finborough Theatre and Carmen subsequently received an OffWestEnd Award nomination for Most Promising New Playwright. In 2018 she was commissioned by Kiln Theatre for their *Mapping Brent* project working with their selected young company to create *Let Kilburn Shake*, directed by Harry Mackrill.

Carmen has been a member of the Orange Tree Writers Collective, the Royal Court Playwriting Group, Hampstead Theatre's Writing the Bigger Picture group, and has an MA in Playwriting from Royal Holloway University. She is currently under commission to the Almeida Theatre, Kiln Theatre and Sky Productions, and is also adapting the Booker-shortlisted novel *Burnt Sugar* by Avni Doshi for The Lot Productions.

Other Original Plays for Young People to Perform from Nick Hern Books

100 Christopher Heimann, Neil Monaghan, Diene Petterle

BANANA BOYS Evan Placey

BOYS Ella Hickson

BRAINSTORM Ned Glasier, Emily Lim and Company Three

BROKEN BISCUITS Tom Wells

BUNNY Jack Thorne

BURYING YOUR BROTHER IN THE PAVEMENT Jack Thorne

THE CHANGING ROOM Chris Bush

CHAOS Laura Lomas

COCKROACH Sam Holcroft

COMMENT IS FREE James Fritz

EIGHT Ella Hickson

THE FALL James Fritz

GIRLS LIKE THAT Evan Placey

HOLLOWAY JONES Evan Placey

THE IT Vivienne Franzmann

OVERSPILL Ali Taylor

PRONOUN Evan Placey

REMOTE Stef Smith

SAME Deborah Bruce

THE SMALL HOURS Katherine Soper

START SWIMMING James Fritz

STUFF Tom Wells

TUESDAY Alison Carr

THE URBAN GIRL'S GUIDE TO CAMPING AND OTHER PLAYS Fin Kennedy

THE WARDROBE Sam Holcroft

WHEN THEY GO LOW Natalie Mitchell

Platform

Platform is a series of plays for young actors with all or mainly female casts, which put young women and their stories at the heart of the action – commissioned by Tonic Theatre, published and licensed by Nick Hern Books.

BRIGHT. YOUNG. THINGS. Georgia Christou

HEAVY WEATHER Lizzie Nunnery

THE GLOVE THIEF Beth Flintoff

THE LIGHT BURNS BLUE Silva Semerciyan

RED Somalia Seaton

SECOND PERSON NARRATIVE Jemma Kennedy

THIS CHANGES EVERYTHING Joel Horwood

For more information, visit www.tonictheatre-platform.co.uk

Carmen Nasr

THE MALADIES

NICK HERN BOOKS

London

www.nickhernbooks.co.uk

A Nick Hern Book

The Maladies first published in Great Britain as a paperback original in 2022 by Nick Hern Books Limited, The Glasshouse, 49a Goldhawk Road, London W12 8QP

The Maladies copyright © 2022 Carmen Nasr

Carmen Nasr has asserted her right to be identified as the author of this work

Cover image: The Other Richard

Designed and typeset by Nick Hern Books, London
Printed in Great Britain by Mimeo Ltd, Huntingdon, Cambridgeshire PE29 6XX

A CIP catalogue record for this book is available from the British Library

ISBN 978 1 84842 994 9

Author's Note
Carmen Nasr

In October 2019, myself, Director Diyan Zora, Associate Director Abi Falase and the Almeida Young Company gathered in a room in London to create a show together. Our starting point was a set of true historical incidents of so called 'mass hysteria'; unexplained outbreaks of dancing, twitching, laughing and fainting. The outbreaks almost exclusively affected young women, particularly those in institutions, in which they had little or almost no power. We asked ourselves: what would an outbreak look like today?

Our rehearsal room soon became one of the most exciting spaces I've worked in. The company were not only deeply creative, thoughtful and generous, but full of courage, joy and passion. We worked hard, we were rigorous and brave and collaborative, it felt special and invigorating. Then on the day we reached a first draft, the pandemic hit and we all went into lockdown.

Across the following two years, we continued to work together at various intervals. Online, or in snatches physically, with masks, without masks; we took long breaks, we redrafted, and we kept trying. The show was scheduled three times and then cancelled three times. A few members left for jobs or drama school. New members joined. It was at times heartbreaking and exhausting, but we all felt the urge to keep coming together, and the Young Company's kindness, care and support for each other never faltered.

I have been astonished and deeply moved by this group of young people, who, when faced with a world that has felt increasingly unsteady, and an industry that is often unkind and unjust, have shown nothing less than the utmost respect and compassion for each other, for themselves and for the work.

They are brave and strong, but also kind and gentle. I have learnt so much from them, and I hope our industry does too.

So, to every single one of the thirty Almeida Young Company members who came together across October 2019 to April 2022 to create *The Maladies*, thank you for your inspiring resilience. We are all so proud of you.

Abdul Sessay, Alice Grant, Anna Rawlings, Anshula Bain, Aubrey Westwood Newman, Daniella Finch, Douglas Clark, Ed Lees, Effie Ansah, Eniola Sunmon, Ethan Joseph-Robert, Francesca Amewudah-Rivers, Helena Alexander, Hosanna Johnson, Iman Boujelouah, Jacob Garvey, Jordan Noel, Josie Charles, Kane Feagan, Kieton Saunders-Browne, Kirsty Williamson, Liam Donnelly, Linda Wachaga, Melanie J Ashurst, Melody Adeniran, Mohamed Manso Bangura, Nicole Caffrey, Patrick Ashe, Priya Kansara, Rawaed Asde.

The Maladies was first performed by the Almeida Young Company at The Yard Theatre, London, on 21 April 2022, with the following cast:

SUSAN	Melody Adeniran
TAMARA	Helena Alexander
CLEO/JORDAN	Effie Ansah
PAUL/FATHER JACOB	Patrick Ashe
MILES	Mohamed Manso Bangura
CLARICE/CLARA	Nicole Caffrey
LEONIE	Josie Charles
DARYL	Douglas Clark
KAYLA	Kane Feagan
OTTO/MR BARKER/	
RYDER HIGH-SCHOOL	
STUDENT	Jake Garvey
ALEX	Alice Grant
MAGDA/MORGAN	Hosanna Johnson
RAFAEL/ACADEMIC 1/	
DR BUSHMAN/FRANK	Ethan Joseph-Robert
ERIC/ACADEMIC 2/	
DR DEREK	Ed Lees
CHRISTINA	Jordan Noel
JESSICA/COURTNEY	Linda Wachaga
RHYS/FRITZ	Aubrey Westwood Newman
IZZY	Kirsty Williamson

All other parts played by members of the company

Director	Yasmin Hafesji
Designer	Grace Venning
Lighting Designer	Fraser Craig
Sound Designer	Kayode Gomez
Movement Director	Ruth Phillips

Associate Director	Abi Falase
Dramaturg	Diyan Zora
Costume Supervisor	Esme Lowrey
Musical Director	Colm Molloy
Producer	Simon Stephens
Assistant Producer	Lauren Joyce-Smith

Notes on the Play

The Podcast takes place in London, in the present, where oppression is often insidious.

The scenes in Strasbourg, Tanzania and Le Roy take place in the imagined past of the podcasters.

Susan and Christina exist beyond time and space.

This text went to press before the end of rehearsals and so may differ slightly from the play as performed.

Characters

MR BARKER, *environmental activist*
JERRY, *mediator*
FRANK, *high-school student*
ERIC, *high-school student*
RYDER, *high-school student*
TV CREW

1500s, 1960s, 2000s AND PODCAST
SUSAN
CHRISTINA

ENSEMBLE
CHOIR, NOTETAKERS, ASSISTANTS, TV CREW,
HIGH-SCHOOL STUDENTS, CHEERLEADERS

Scene One

As the audience enters the theatre an episode of the
Empowercast *podcast plays. Perhaps it plays in the bar or the*
foyer as they wait to enter the space. Maybe the audience can
even download the podcast and listen to it on their journey to
the theatre or before they come to watch the play.

The podcast episode is improvised and recorded by the actors
playing CLEO, JESSICA, TAMARA *and* LEONIE. *Maybe*
IZZY *and* MILES *have a cameo. At some point they discuss and*
debate the feminist merits of the song 'WAP', by Cardi B (feat.
Megan Thee Stallion).

As the audience takes their seats the podcast episode continues
to play until the lights go down and the audience falls silent.

At some point the podcasters play the song 'WAP'.

As the song plays, the lights go up to reveal SUSAN,
CHRISTINA, MAGDA *and* CLARICE *in full 1500s attire*
kneading dough. The song continues to play. It's strenuous work.
They knead and knead and knead as clouds of flour puff up
around them.

TIME AND SPACE GLITCHES AND SHIFTS.

Scene Two

London. Trilogy Media's central London offices. A recording
studio on the 21st floor. The room is soundproofed. It's at once
extremely corporate and also obnoxiously hip. The room is set
up to record a podcast, perhaps the microphones hang from
the ceiling, or sprout out from the ground. The room is full of

*the trappings of Silicon Valley start-up culture, maybe there's
free snacks, coffee machine, mini-fridge of craft beer, branded
jellybeans, etc.*

LEONIE, JESSICA, CLEO, TAMARA, IZZY *and* MILES *are
led in by* ALEX

DARYL. Wow. I can't believe you are finally here! Welcome
to Trilogy! We are huge *Empowercast* fans, I've listened to
every single episode, I feel like I've known you all my life,
like we're best friends, and we are so pumped aren't we
Alex?

ALEX. Yeah.

ALEX *goes back to her iPad and swipes and types
throughout most of the scene.*

DARYL. Leonie, Jessica, Chloe –

CLEO. Cleo.

DARYL. Cleo, Izzy, Tamara, Miles. Welcome to the Trilogy
family! Okay, so here at Trilogy we always start the day with
a feelings circle. Right, Alex?

ALEX. Yeah.

DARYL *ushers them into a circle.* ALEX *does this while still
swiping on her iPad.*

DARYL. Okay. So one word. Let's do – if your current feeling
was a fruit what would it be? I'll start. Melon.

A slightly awkward pause, until LEONIE *realises she's next.*

LEONIE. Oh me? Erm… A grape?

CLEO. Mango.

MILES. A banana.

JESSICA. Okay. A pineapple.

IZZY. Plum.

DARYL. Alex?

ALEX. Oh. Sorry. Kumquat.

DARYL. Great! So Alex has a few documents for you to sign now that you're finally in the building, so we'll leave you to it for a second and be back soon to talk ideas for the new season – help yourselves to the jellybeans!

ALEX and DARYL exit. As soon as they leave, the podcasters scream with excitement and fist-pump the air, etc.

TAMARA. This is so cool!

JESSICA. I can't believe we're actually here.

CLEO. I know, this is epic!

IZZY. These jellybeans are flavourless.

MILES. I just want to say well done, guys, I mean look at this. Look how far you've come. I'm just happy to be here with you!

CLEO. Thanks, Miles. Let's take a first-day selfie!

They take a selfie. Some of them start signing the contract straight away, as others read through it.

JESSICA. Guys, it says here that we can't say 'the tits' on the podcast –

LEONIE. Who cares!

MILES. Have you seen how much our sign-on bonus is?

TAMARA. There's a champagne tap?! This can't be real; it has to be a joke –

ALEX and DARYL return, and ALEX starts collecting the signed contracts.

ALEX. – that's for external clients only.

DARYL. Right, let's get stuck into some ideas for the season. Why don't we all take turns to pitch an idea? Who wants to start?

An ASSISTANT/NOTETAKER has also entered, we almost

don't notice them come in. The ASSISTANT *is almost always there, and almost always a different person. If they aren't taking notes, they are just around fixing things, rearranging jellybeans, restocking beer, etc. During the brainstorm, it's* ALEX *who takes notes on a high-tech whiteboard, or something that can be seen by the audience.*

JESSICA. Oh, I'm so sorry, Daryl, but we already have an idea all ready to go for the new season. We usually take turns, and this season is my turn.

DARYL. Oh, I'm sorry, of course.

JESSICA. Izzy and I've got heaps of research that we think will really resonate with our –

DARYL. Oh my God, totally, I mean the last thing I want to do is come in here and like try and change the way you do things. Right?

JESSICA. Okay, great.

DARYL. The thing is Adam, our CEO, has a certain way of doing things and he insists on brainstorms for all new seasons, no exceptions. It's about harnessing diversity of thought for inclusive decision making, eliminating groupthink. All good? Let's go!

The podcasters are caught a bit off guard and are silent for just over what is comfortable.

So, who wants to jump in first?

JESSICA. I'll go. We were already thinking about curating a season around the menstruation cycle. It would follow the various stages of the cycle –

ALEX *writes something a bit ridiculous like 'period chat'.*

DARYL. That sounds great, Jessica. Who's next? Iggy?

IZZY. It's Izzy.

DARYL. Of course. Izzy.

IZZY *thinks.*

IZZY. Can you come back to me?

CLEO. Erm, okay. What about endometriosis?

TAMARA. Or period poverty.

MILES. Tampon tax?

They've already run out of steam.

DARYL. These are all sounding quite gynecological –

LEONIE. What about fetishes? It's always about the white male fetish. So we could explore like unusual fetishes, from diverse perspectives –

DARYL. I love it. Tell me more. Let's hear an example.

LEONIE *can't think of anything.* CLEO *jumps in to save her.*

CLEO. Okay. So. My friend's friend's cousin, right, her husband has like a bit of a breast-feeding fetish, like he always wanted to suck her boobs and stuff. She didn't mind at first but then like it got weird and he started like drinking a pint of milk before and after sex, calling her 'mamacita' and shit...

DARYL. Oh wow. Okay. What else have we got?

ALEX *has written 'Milky Sex'. The podcasters try not to panic.*

IZZY. My cousin used to be a stripper.

DARYL. Erm, okay. Great. Anyone else?

An awkward silence. It goes on for longer than is comfortable. LEONIE *suddenly remembers –*

LEONIE. Oh my God! What about that Slackerz story you were telling us about, Jessica?

DARYL. Slackerz as in *Slackerz Media?*

LEONIE. Yeah, so, Jessica has a friend of a friend at Slackerz – her name's Susan right? Out of nowhere, she totally lost her voice, for a full month now –

JESSICA. Oh yeah, and since Susan went silent, four more women have too – all from the marketing team. No matter how hard they try – they literally just can't speak.

LEONIE. They've brought in the best private doctors and even they can't figure out what's causing it or how it's spreading.

CLEO. That's *mega* freaky.

TAMARA. Sounds like a super-toxic workplace to me.

IZZY. What if it's some sort of curse?

LEONIE. Apparently, they're desperate to keep the whole story quiet.

JESSICA. I'm telling you it's a hundred per cent something in the water. I mean the KPMG water-cooler scandal was only last year, it wreaked havoc on female employees' menstrual cycles, excessive cramps, bleeding, it was awful. It took them a whole year to even bother to test the water and find that chemical leak.

LEONIE. We could be breaking a huge scandal here.

CLEO. It could work.

LEONIE. We could investigate why the hell this silence is happening, talk to the victims –

ALEX. But they can't speak.

LEONIE. What do you think, Daryl?

A moment of and anticipation before DARYL *breaks his silence.*

DARYL. It's not just a season. It is GENIUS! Adam is going to go crazy for this silence thing. Let's do this!

JESSICA. That wasn't exactly the plan.

LEONIE. But this story does feel exciting. Right, guys?

The podcasters all agree with varying levels of enthusiasm.

DARYL. Great! It's like investigative true crime with a side of sexy feminist banter.

ALEX. That is totally Adam's vibe.

DARYL. Are those contracts all signed? Amazing!

TIME AND SPACE GLITCHES AND SHIFTS.

Scene Three

Strasbourg, 1518. Two young women, SUSAN *and*
CHRISTINA, *are kneading dough in a bakery. They wear long
full dresses of the era, the imagined clothes of an imagined past.
It's pre-dawn, the whole city is asleep, this is the time when
women are alone, when women talk together. We might hear the
sound of church bells.*

CHRISTINA. And you're sure it said we're allowed to go?

SUSAN. My Frank read it out to me. Loud and clear. It said:
    'Church Meeting. Topic: The Dancing Plague and What to
    Do About It'. Then in small print it said: 'Women Welcome'.

CHRISTINA. Wow.

SUSAN. Then in brackets: Temporarily.

CHRISTINA. Women welcome. Wow.

SUSAN. Things are changing. Us women, we're on the up,
    Christina.

CHRISTINA. Easy, now.

SUSAN. I'm going to that meeting and you and the others are
    all coming with me.

CHRISTINA. What? No we're not! And don't mention a word
    of this to them, they're gossips, especially Clarice.

SUSAN. I need you all there. We'll be stronger in numbers.

CHRISTINA. What the hell do we need to be strong for?

    SUSAN *looks around to see the coast is clear.*

SUSAN. Because I'm going to speak.

CHRISTINA. Speak?! Are you mad? We aren't allowed to
    speak in public and what the hell do you have to say anyway?

    MAGDA *and* CLARICE *enter and get to work, they all
    knead together.*

MAGDA. Twenty-seven people and counting, this is a proper plague now.

CLARICE. We saw a group of them on the way in, writhing around like rats, but in rhythm.

MAGDA. Did you hear?
There's some sort of emergency meeting and apparently they're letting women attend. Controversial.

CLARICE. My mother's horrified. She said a public meeting is no place for a lady. Said it's shameful.

MAGDA. They're so stuck in their ways our mothers. Mine is so repressed she still insists on going to confession everyday.

They roll their eyes and scoff at the how regressive this is.

I've tried to explain to her that us modern women only go three times a week.

CHRISTINA. If that.

They laugh at how naughty this is. They knead in unison.

SUSAN. Women welcome. Don't you like the sound of that? So I was thinking –

CHRISTINA. Talking of confession, how was Father Jacob yesterday, Clarice?

MAGDA. Was he a bit handsy?

CLARICE. Oh yeah. You know what he's like.
But I don't mind really.

CHRISTINA. Poor man. Can't help himself.

MAGDA. He's lovely really.

The others agree. They knead.

SUSAN. Women welcome. Think about it. It's a new era. And I can see a new dawn breaking through. It's bright and it's glittering. Imagine the places our daughters will go.

Dawn has arrived, it starts to rise behind them. The future, for a moment, is female.

SUSAN. And this meeting right –

CHRISTINA. You know I had a crazy idea on my way in here. So this whole kneading method here, what if we sort of expanded it.

CHRISTINA demonstrates by sitting on the floor, her legs wide open and kneads the dough in between her legs. CLARICE and MAGDA watch on in horror.

This really opens up the movement. This way we expand it so we can really put our back into it. And it's alright because look my dress still covers the ankles. See? I've got so much power now, all that power going into the bread, look at that space, look at that bread. This is the future of breadmaking right here, it's all in this angle, it's all here, look at that power.

CLARICE. Absolutely not. We'll stick to how we've always done it. Thank you.

CHRISTINA. You're right. Sometimes I get carried away. Get these crazy ideas. I don't know what I was thinking. This is much better.

CHRISTINA is now back up kneading at the table with the other women. They continue kneading in silence.

SUSAN. So is anyone going to the meeting?

There is a chorus of disapproval, 'Oh no's, 'Good God's, 'Bit much', etc…

I am. I'm going.

A silence falls on the women.

MAGDA. What the hell for?

SUSAN. I need you all to come with me. You see I think I know why this is happening, the dancing, I have to tell them.

CLARICE. She's lost her marbles. Gets invited to one meeting and thinks she's Joan of bloody Arc.

MAGDA. The devil's in them that's why they're dancing.

CLARICE. Doctor says they've got hot blood.

MAGDA. We all know what that means. That they enjoy it.

CLARICE. And no one should enjoy sex.

SUSAN looks around and lowers her voice.

SUSAN. Listen I think it started here. The dancing. With the bread. With our bread.

CLARICE. Don't be stupid. What you talking about?

SUSAN. Frau Troffea, the first woman, the first dancer, the morning she started it all, came here for bread. It smelt strange that day, not off exactly, just weird. She asks for her usual order and she walks off with her baguettes, but after just a few steps, she stops and takes a bite.

CLARICE. Fat cow

SUSAN. Immediately her leg starts to jig. Her arms swaying her hips swinging back and forth. And that's when it all started. And the second woman to dance. Frau Gretchen. She bought three baguettes that same day. And two pastries. And ten biscuits. And a cream puff.

And the third. Frau Flora, she bought two baguettes and a loaf of rye.

CHRISTINA. Good God. What if she's right? What if the bread's cursed?

One of the women has been chewing on a baguette, as it dawns on her that the bread might be cursed, she stops chewing and quietly tries to spit out the bread into her hand.

SUSAN. They aren't possessed. And it's not hot blood. Or madness. It's the bread – we have to help them.

ERIC enters with a delivery of flour.

ERIC. Morning, ladies.

They say their good mornings in return.

Hi, Christina. You alright?

CHRISTINA. Hi, Eric. I like your flour sacks, are they new?

ERIC. Thank you. Yeah. They are.

ERIC and CHRISTINA *grin at each other.*

CLARICE. Get on with it, Eric, we haven't got all day.

ERIC snaps out of it and starts unloading the flour.

MAGDA. Those bells haven't stopped all morning.

ERIC. Haven't you heard? Poor Frau Gretchen, she's danced herself to death.

The women are horrified.

Collapsed right in the middle of the square. I happened to be passing and they sent me to get Father Jacob. To do the last rites and all that. But he got there too late. Couldn't even save her soul.

A SHIFT IN TIME AND SPACE.

Scene Four

Trilogy Media's offices. JESSICA, MILES, IZZY *and* TAMARA *are in the room, waiting for everyone to arrive, they seem a bit more comfortable in their new surroundings, but not yet totally at home.*

MILES. Oh my god, Jessica, you're trending, people are tweeting about your water theory.

JESSICA. Like, actually trending? Let me see.

MILES. Yeah look #TEAMJESSICA.

CLEO. I'm sorry, why isn't there a #TEAMCLEO.

TAMARA. Who cares! We are trending!

JESSICA. I'm telling you guys the people are always right. There's something in that damn water.

CLEO. We're gonna be famous, I'm telling you. One episode in and this shit is trending and you're like a modern-day Greta fucking Thunberg.

MILES. No way! Is this for real? Adam, like big-man Adam upstairs, just followed me! From his personal account.

JESSICA. What? He hasn't followed me.

TAMARA. Or me. You're not even a host.

They check their phones to make sure.

CLEO. He's literally only followed Miles. You're just the techie, we had to like beg them to let you come here with us.

MILES. Wait, what?

TAMARA. Have you guys ever seen Adam? Like in the flesh?

JESSICA. Who cares, he's just a corporate suit like the rest of them.

IZZY. Apparently he only drinks coconut water instead of, like, water water.

JESSICA. Sounds like a bit of a dick dick.

MILES. I actually kinda like the guy.

JESSICA. You've literally never met him.

TAMARA. He did buy our podcast so he can't be a complete dick.

JESSICA. Sell-out.

TAMARA. Sorry to break it to you but you sold out the minute you signed that contract.

LEONIE *enters, her hands are full with her laptop, maybe some notebooks.*

LEONIE. I've just spoken to our source at Slackerz and the cases have tripled since last week. TRIPLED!

CLEO. That's like fifteen people? This is like proper plague shit, now.

LEONIE. And the new cases are all in the HR department, which is on the floor directly above marketing. And get this they're all women, that can't be a random coincidence, right?

A NOTETAKER *enters. They walk in and take their place. Maybe they take out a laptop, or refill the bowl of jellybeans. The podcasters watch on, bemused.*

TAMARA. Hi.

NOTETAKER. Hi.

LEONIE. Okay so Izzy did some amazing research and she's found all these unexplained weird outbreaks from the past, so I thought we could add another layer and you know draw on history as we investigate. So first up there was this dancing plague in the sixteenth century.

IZZY enters with her tea and sits down at her desk.

IZZY. Yeah, it was in Strasbourg back in 1518 –

JESSICA. Are you okay?

They exchange looks for a second.

IZZY. It's just a sore throat.

CLEO. Well just don't go falling silent and shit, Izzy.

IZZY. Honestly, I'm fine. Anyway, I've been researching this dancing plague in Strasbourg back in 1518. This woman, out of nowhere, starts dancing and dancing – it's compulsive. They just can't stop. Within a week, forty-five women have joined her. Eventually, it spreads to hundreds of people and they start dying from heart attacks and strokes –

TAMARA. Jesus.

IZZY. So the city decide they can be cured by having them just dance it out of their system. You can just imagine it, this ancient town, with its cobbled streets and church spires in the middle of this… plague. They gather in the evenings with this choir, and as the sun sets…

TIME AND SPACE SHIFT.

1518, a twenty-person choir stands in Strasbourg town square, or maybe its cathedral. They sing 'WAP', by Cardi B (feat. Megan Thee Stallion) in Latin. IZZY listens with her eyes closed.

TIME AND SPACE GLITCHES AND SHIFTS.

We return to the studio. Time has shifted forward. The team is mid-recording. DARYL and ALEX have appeared.

TAMARA. Nah, I just don't buy Slackerz has had their water poisoned or Leonie's psychological angle. It sounds like a throat disease – have they tried honey, ginger and lemon?

LEONIE. Honey and ginger, are you serious, Tamara?

CLEO. What if it's stress related? Slight tangent. My cousin's friend works in marketing in this huge marketing company, she's on like eighty grand a year. Eighty grand a year to sit on her arse! Anyway, not the point. Basically, her boss was a proper tyrant. Always on her back, always making her do the tiniest little thing. Eventually, the stress got so bad that her hair started falling out. In clumps! Alopecia –

LEONIE. Remember at uni when we had to do those presentations, I swear for days beforehand I'd get actual headaches from the nerves.

CLEO. I'm telling you stress and anxiety can do mad shit to your body –

MILES. I remember Cleo had such bad nerves she used to give her presentations wasted, like that time when she'd had four pints before a seminar and –

CLEO. Lol, you can you talk... lest we forget... chicken-gate! Miles turned up to a party in a chicken costume, got so wasted that he took the costume off IN WINTER – in the cold and rain. My man wasn't wearing any underwear! We saw all his little chicken bits and it wasn't pretty –

DARYL turns off the recording light.

DARYL. So sorry to cut you guys off. We love the flow you guys have, we love the back and forth, all that's great, it's mega exciting, just could you go a little slower?

LEONIE. Like speak slower?

DARYL. It's just that we're trying to grow that older listener demographic, and boomers, well, they're not used to like 'urban' voices, just a bit more of a breath before you speak –

CLEO and MILES *exchange a glance.*

CLEO. What do you mean by 'urban' –

ALEX. There was also the other note from Adam?

JESSICA. W-w-wait… how many notes are there?

DARYL. That's right. It's really hard to understand you at times, Jessica. You've got a slight stutter, so if we could just get that under control that would be great. I'm sure we can get someone at Trilogy to get it checked out for you.

JESSICA. Okay.

CLEO. Okay?

DARYL. Great stuff.

They go back to recording.

JESSICA. So you really think there might be a psychological angle here?

CLEO. A hundred per cent. If it was physical they would have figured it out by now, right?

JESSICA. I absolutely disagree.

CLEO. And why's that?

JESSICA. I know I'm a chatterbox now, but when I was a kid I had a stutter. A really bad stutter. Enough to not have any friends because it took me three minutes to finish a sentence. Enough to have food thrown at me on the top floor of the bus. Enough to eat lunch alone every day for five years. But when I was fourteen, my cousin took me to my first protest. I remember standing in the crowd, everyone was chanting, all at once, and I could feel the ground vibrating. It made me feel held and strong, and then I started chanting, and for the first time in my life I didn't stutter, like Colin Firth in that *King's Speech* movie, and it sounds so cringe but that's how it stopped, that's how I found my voice, and now these women have lost theirs – like, literally – and no one gives a shit, so I'm giving my voice up in solidarity.

JESSICA *takes out some duct tape.*

Because I know what it's like not to have one. I'm taking a vow of silence until they test the water at Slackerz.

JESSICA *tapes her mouth shut.*

TIME AND SPACE GLITCHES AND SHIFTS.

Scene Five

1518, Strasbourg. The Church. FATHER JACOB *presides over a meeting of town councillors.* SUSAN *and* CHRISTINA *are penned into a special area for the temporarily invited women. The councillors,* ERIC, FRITZ, OTTO *and* RAFAEL, *are in a heated debate. Perhaps* CLARICE *and* MAGDA *are secretly watching from a window.*

FRITZ. What if we just tie up their ankles.

OTTO. They've been showing too much of them anyway.

RAFAEL. Fritz, that's an absurd idea.

FRITZ. Otto's right – those dresses are shorter every year, it's a disgrace –

OTTO. It'll be shins and elbows next –

ERIC. – What if we build a stage, invite an audience, and let them dance it out.

The men think ERIC *and his suggestion are ridiculous.*

Just hear me out. We get some musicians, maybe a choir, I know a great flautist, a personal friend actually –

RAPHAEL. A young woman has died, this is not the time for some deranged shindig.

FRITZ. Five years ago there was only the Bible, and now with this printing press, there's hundreds of books, foreign stories, filth.

RAPHAEL. I have heard that some of the women have secretly been learning to read.

FRITZ. Well then, we should burn the books. Or maybe we should burn some of the women –

OTTO. You can't burn books! That's barbaric –

RAFAEL. How about we ban women from leaving their homes? From congregating together –

FRITZ. It's demonic possession. You can see it in their eyes. What about a mass exorcism, Father Jacob?

ERIC. I really think we've got to just help them dance it all out, stage, music, maybe even some costumes –

OTTO. How is more dancing going to help in a dancing epidemic?

ERIC. Maybe we should ask the women what they think?

ERIC*'s suggestion sends the men into uproar as they argue among themselves* SUSAN *steps over the barrier and walks towards the men. She stops and stands in front of them and* FATHER JACOB. *When they notice her, they all fall silent and stare.*

SUSAN. It's the bread, Father.

FATHER JACOB. Excuse me?

SUSAN. It's the bread, it's making them ill. Making them dance.

FATHER JACOB. Women are not permitted to speak in the church. Or in the townhall. Or the schoolhouse, or anywhere, really.

SUSAN. I wish I didn't have to speak. To shame myself like this, but I know the truth and I have to speak it. It's the bread.

FATHER JACOB. You haven't been to confession in months, woman.

SUSAN. And I stand before you in sin.

FATHER JACOB. If you want to speak here. In public. I must hear your sins.

SUSAN. What? Now?

FATHER JACOB. Yes, child. Then you may speak.

SUSAN. Here? In front of all these people?

FATHER JACOB. Yes. May the Lord be in your heart and help you to confess your sins with true sorrow. What are your sins, child?

SUSAN. Forgive me, Father, for I have sinned...

FATHER JACOB. Well what is it? What are your sins?

SUSAN. All of them?

FATHER JACOB. All of them.

SUSAN. Well, yesterday I ate two portions instead of one.

FATHER JACOB. One Hail Mary.

SUSAN *twitches.*

SUSAN. I said something stupid to my father and didn't apologise.

FATHER JACOB. Two Hail Marys.

SUSAN. I let a man buy me a drink at the tavern that I didn't really want but said yes anyway.

She twitches again. The twitching increases with each line of dialogue.

FATHER JACOB. Four Hail Marys.

SUSAN. I tried on a pair of my brother's trousers.

FATHER JACOB. Eight Hail Marys.

SUSAN. I cried for no reason, at the dinner table, and upset the children.
I used my Bible as a doorstop.
And I found deep unimaginable pleasure in reproductive activities with my husband.

FATHER JACOB. One hundred Hail Marys!

SUSAN'S *twitching becomes dancing.*

She can't control it.

She dances and dances and dances.

TIME AND SPACES SHIFTS.

Scene Six

Trilogy Media's offices. LEONIE, TAMARA, CLEO *and* JESSICA *are at their microphones.* JESSICA *still has her mouth taped shut, she's accessorised the tape with some stickers, she's even got a mini home-made cardboard protest sign, it reads 'LISTEN TO WOMEN'S BODIES'.* MILES *sits in his place.* DARYL *and* ALEX *enter.*

LEONIE. Tamara, Cleo, please can you talk some sense into her?

DARYL. No don't do that. It's absolutely genius, last week's listener rates were through the roof.

IZZY *enters.*

LEONIE. How's your sore throat, Izzy?

IZZY *walks over to her desk and sits down without saying a word.*

MILES. Shit are you okay?

IZZY *stares at them for a few moments. She opens her mouth to speak, but nothing comes out.*

IZZY. Just joking!

CLEO. Fucking hell, Izzy, you freaked me out.

IZZY. I told you it was nothing.

DARYL. Okay, gang. So, Rhys and Carla.

ALEX. Kayla.

DARYL. Thanks. Rhys and Kayla are on their way up.

CLEO. Who's Kayla?

ALEX. Susan's colleague.

LEONIE. Why couldn't we get Susan?

ALEX. Health and safety. She could be contagious.

DARYL. Can we park this conversation and focus on the strategy with Rhys and Kayla? They will have been extensively briefed so you've got to go hard.

CLEO. It's actually not really our thing to 'go hard'.

DARYL. You know what I mean. Make them squirm.

IZZY. That sounds painful –

DARYL. Look, you need to be tactful with these people. Just dial the heat up a bit when it feels appropriate and let them sizzle.

TAMARA. We don't want to make them feel pressured into –

DARYL. Totally agree. But these women are getting seriously sick.

LEONIE. He's got a point. If we don't dig for information, who will?

TAMARA. Fine, we'll push. A little.

ALEX. They're at reception.

DARYL. I'll bring them through. Warm them up for you a little.

DARYL *exits*.

LEONIE. I hope we can get something out of them on Slackerz.

ALEX (*to* MILES). I used to intern at Slackerz.

MILES. Oh, really, that's nice –

LEONIE. – What? Why didn't you say anything before?

ALEX. Bit handsy.

LEONIE. I knew it. Can you be more specific, what exactly do you mean by 'handsy'?

ALEX. Just a bit handsy.

CLEO. Okay, why are you only saying this now, Alex?

DARYL walks in with RHYS and KAYLA, cutting off the conversation.

DARYL. Rhys and Kayla, everyone.

TIME AND SPACE GLITCHES AND SHIFTS.

Microphones fall into place. We are now mid-recording.

LEONIE. So, Rhys, how is Susan?

RHYS. She's doing well, yeah.

TAMARA. And how are you managing to communicate?

RHYS. Well, I bought her a notebook with her initials on the front and that's how she talks to me now.

TAMARA. That must be tough for you both –

RHYS. It's actually quite cute, she does little doodles of animals instead of names and I'm this tiny puppy with –

LEONIE. Do you think her job might have a role to play, here? Perhaps the stress –

RHYS. Look it's really important to emphasise that this is absolutely something physical, not psychological or emotional.

LEONIE. If it was physical surely it would have been detected by now.

RHYS. Some of your listeners are saying it's some sort of hysteria, which is incredibly patronising and, frankly, sexist.

LEONIE. Okay, but –

RHYS. Like, imagine you woke up one day and out of the blue you were mute, or deaf, or blind, and then people started telling you it was all in your head.

KAYLA. Exactly. And Slackerz is a great place to work. I mean sure, it's hard work which can lead to stress –

LEONIE. What kind of stress?

KAYLA. The usual work stress, you know, endless emails and meetings.

LEONIE. Are you aware of recent reports detailing a culture of 'handsyness' at Slackerz?

KAYLA. That's ridiculous.

LEONIE. Well, there have been first-hand accounts reported –

KAYLA. Reported or rumoured?

LEONIE. Reported. Kayla, these are first-hand accounts from –

KAYLA. I have no idea what you're talking about.

LEONIE. Then let me explain, there have been multiple reports from different women –

KAYLA. Is this why you've brought me on here? To respond to rumours?

LEONIE. No, we –

KAYLA. Have you got any evidence to back up these claims?

LEONIE. Erm, well, not exactly but we do have –

KAYLA. We're meant to be talking about Susan, to raise awareness about the silence, and you're trying to smear Slackerz with false allegations –

CLEO. Why we don't take five?

KAYLA. There's really no need

The recording light goes off.

CLEO. Okay, Kayla. We're not recording. Anything you say is off record.

KAYLA. Off record?

CLEO. Totally off record.

The recording light goes on. No one in the room notices. It's clear to the audience that it's DARYL *who is behind it.*

Take your time.

KAYLA. There's really nothing to say.

CLEO. I know what it's like to be in a toxic workplace.

KAYLA. I really don't know anything about these allegations.

CLEO. Remember, this is all off-mic.

KAYLA. Look, all I can say is that I've had an incredibly positive experience at Slackerz. I haven't seen any 'handsyness' or whatever you're calling it.

LEONIE. Well, Alex here used to intern at Slackerz, and she says otherwise.

ALEX. I didn't say anything like that.

LEONIE. You said it was handsy.

ALEX. No I didn't…

LEONIE. Yes you did. Like literally ten minutes ago.

ALEX. I absolutely did not say that.

LEONIE. Alex, you said it was handsy.

ALEX. I don't know what you're talking about, Leonie.

LEONIE. Seriously, Alex. It's okay. We're off-mic.

ALEX *goes back to her iPad.*

KAYLA. She's telling you nothing happened. Why are you pushing?

LEONIE. I'm not pushing, she said –

KAYLA. This so-called feminist speculation – or whatever it is – is what's really doing the damage.

LEONIE. It's not speculation though, is it, there's –

KAYLA. If there's no trauma, stop looking for it.

LEONIE. We're just keeping all angles open –

KAYLA. Listen, the more you speculate about stress, made-up trauma, and psychological issues, the more it delays us finding out what is going on with Susan and the rest of my colleagues at Slackerz.

CLEO. Some people think it might be some form of protest, a group of women going silent, that's a powerful statement.

KAYLA. There's no way in hell a women would sacrifice her voice to make a point.

JESSICA *starts writing in her notebook.*

No offence.

CLEO. She's trying to write something. Oh no, wait, her pen isn't working, LOL.

KAYLA. But you're a bit ridiculous. I can't believe you're sitting there taping your mouth shut when Susan and the other women have no choice. It's insulting.

CLEO *leans over and reads our what she's writing.*

CLEO. She says 'Fuck this I'm gonna talk'.

JESSICA *takes off the duct tape. It looks painful. The others wince. She holds her mouth for a few seconds to ease the pain. She takes in a deep breath to speak. She can't. She tries again. She can't. She panics. The others stare in horror.*

TIME AND SPACE GLITCHES.

She gestures to them for some sort of help. LEONIE *gets up and goes to* JESSICA. *At the same time* CLEO *notices that the recording light is on.*

TIME AND SPACE SHIFTS.

Scene Seven

*As time and space glitch from the previous scene, we hear
distorted extracts of the podcast as we move through time to
1962 in the newly formed Tanzania.*

A CHOIR OF SCHOOL CHILDREN *in a mission-run boarding
school sings 'The Locomotion' by Little Eva in a mixture of
Swahili and English in perfect harmony.* SUSAN *stands in the
centre of the choir.*

TIME AND SPACE GLITCHES.

*One of the choir members stops singing and stares ahead in
horror as if they've seen something terrifying.*

TIME AND SPACE GLITCHES.

*What could be a devil or a demon appears for just a second in
the choir. The choir members scream in horror.*

TIME AND SPACE GLITCHES.

They sing in perfect unison as if nothing happened. SUSAN
*starts to giggle. Soon another person catches the giggles. Soon
everyone is laughing uncontrollably. The laughing goes on and
on until it becomes a bit uncomfortable.*

TIME AND SPACE SHIFTS.

Scene Eight

LEONIE, CLEO *and* TAMARA *are present.* JESSICA*'s little
protest sign still sits there.* IZZY *sits at her research desk; she
has lots of papers and books stacked up around her.* MILES *is
also in his place.* DARYL *and* ALEX *stand.*

DARYL. We're so sorry about Jessica.

ALEX. We sent her a fruit basket.

DARYL. We sent her a fruit basket. Look, I know this must be quite a difficult time for you. Why don't I lead a feelings circle? We can each say one word to describe how we feel. I'll start.

I feel... ready. Iggy?

IZZY. It's Izzy. Erm... Perplexed I guess?

MILES. A bit upset.

CLEO. Terrified. Obviously.

TAMARA. Unsettled.

ALEX. Is hungover a feeling?

LEONIE. We're all really upset about Jessica. But we're also pissed off that you kept recording when we'd promised our guests we were off-mic. It's a total violation of trust.

DARYL. Okay. So firstly I am so so so sorry, that you feel that way. Please be angry. Trust your outrage. However, when you said off-mic, I thought you meant like 'Off-mic'.

IZZY. What are you talking about?

DARYL. At Trilogy, there isn't really an off-mic per se, because technically everything that is said in all our recording studios, legally speaking, belongs to Trilogy.

TAMARA. I don't remember being told that.

DARYL. Well it's in your contract.

CLEO. I don't remember that.

DARYL. Small print – it's easy to miss –

ALEX. Can we get on with recording episode four? We're already behind, and this is just wasting more time.

CLEO. I don't feel right about carrying on without Jessica.

DARYL. Right, well that's tricky because you're legally contracted for a full season.

LEONIE. Jessica did say that she wants us to carry on. Well, that's what she texted.

CLEO. Of course she's gonna say that but, look, I don't know. I feel weird about it.

ALEX. She's not dead.

DARYL. Why don't you take some time to talk this through together? I've got a meeting in five, but we can touch base after?

DARYL *and* ALEX *exit.*

TAMARA. I guess he sort of apologised?

CLEO. Did he? Because I didn't hear one. I think we should stop the podcast until –

TAMARA. If we stop then we could lose everything.

CLEO. Not stop stop, like, just a break.

LEONIE. I don't think they'll let us have a break.

CLEO. Jessica's gone silent, doesn't that scare you?

TAMARA. We don't know exactly what's –

CLEO. Even before Jessica left, it hasn't felt right here. It feels like we can't truly express ourselves on our own podcast. Like it's not our voice anymore?

TAMARA. But that's just because we're new and Daryl –

IZZY. Has *so many opinions* –

TAMARA. Once we land our second season, we'll be calling the shots.

CLEO. There's only so much more of this I can take. I feel like I wanna just walk now and –

TAMARA. And go where?

CLEO. I don't know. Back to my old job.

TAMARA. Seriously? Your old boss was way worse than Daryl and it paid shit.

CLEO. Are you blind? This place is toxic.

TAMARA. Are you serious, Cleo?

LEONIE. It's not that bad, is it?

CLEO. Yeah, guys. Fuck the contracts. Strength in numbers. Let's go back to doing it like we did before. Independent. No dumb notes from Adam.

IZZY. I think we sold the mics.

CLEO. Miles has a friend with studio space.

TAMARA. Are you genuinely considering leaving? Come on.

LEONIE. We're just discussing our options.

TAMARA. I don't have any fucking options. You know Trilogy are sponsoring my visa. We talked about this. We all agreed.

CLEO. I'm sure we can sort something out.

TAMARA. You don't understand! Visas don't just appear out of thin air. Do you know how rare it is for a company to sponsor you? Is Miles' friend going to sponsor me from his studio space? Are you? My whole life is here. I can't just leave because Jessica decided to try and save the world again.

MILES. That's a low blow, Tamara. She's gone silent –

TAMARA. I know, sorry, I didn't mean that.

CLEO. If Jessica's got it any one of us could be next.

LEONIE. Surely if you're scared of catching silence in an outbreak, the worst thing you can do is stop talking.

IZZY. Leonie's right.

TAMARA. I don't really have much of a choice. Please, Cleo?

CLEO. Fine. I'll stay. On one condition. Episode four I get to do my piece on Tanzania.

A SHIFT IN TIME AND SPACE.

Scene Nine

1962. Tanzania. Bukoba State radio station. The radio jingle is a Tanzanian version of 'The Locomotion'. Two ACADEMICS *are recording a public health broadcast.* SUSAN *and her* CHRISTINA *are listening. They make faces accordingly.*

ACADEMIC 1. This is a public health announcement.

ACADEMIC 2. We have identified an outbreak of abnormal emotional behavior among the schoolgirls of Tanzania, which has disrupted life in our communities for three months now.

ACADEMIC 1. Behaviours include attacks of laughing and crying, which last from a few minutes to a few hours. Three hundred and seventy girls between twelve and eighteen are affected, in addition to one teacher.

ACADEMIC 2. The onset is sudden and appears to follow contact with another victim. We are testing the water and food supply.

ACADEMIC 1. However, we are unsure of the cause. So in the meantime we have drawn up some guidelines.

BOTH. ADVICE TO THE MOTHERS OF TANZANIA

ACADEMIC 2. Avoid all jokes with your daughters. Puns included.

ACADEMIC 1. Do not speak to your daughters about their futures or their dreams.

ACADEMIC 2. Distract them with household chores that will make them bored and tired.

ACADEMIC 1. Do not let them drink the water. Find alternative sources of hydration.

ACADEMIC 2. This could potentially be a case of spiritual possession.

ACADEMIC 1. As a precaution, read the Bible to your children every night –

ACADEMIC 2. But avoid any of the funny parts.

ACADEMIC 1. We know you may want to hug or comfort your child.

ACADEMIC 2. But we urge you not to empathise with your daughters too much.

ACADEMIC 1. As we believe this may cause contagion to yourself or others.

ACADEMIC 2. You can do this by thinking of their faults and the things that you dislike in their personalities.

ACADEMIC 1. The things they have done that have embarrassed or shamed you.

ACADEMIC 2. Or think of the dreams you had to give up by birthing them.

ACADEMIC 1. Tell them serious stories with a deep moral dimension.

ACADEMIC 2. This helps counteract their frivolous natures.

ACADEMIC 1. Don't tell them we are a free country now.

ACADEMIC 2. Don't explain the politics.

ACADEMIC 1. Too much independence can be destabilising.

ACADEMIC 2. Keep their feet on the ground.

ACADEMIC 1. They may seek attention and fake symptoms so keep a close eye.

ACADEMIC 2. Don't laugh at their jokes.

ACADEMIC 1. But if they look sad.

ACADEMIC 2. It's still safe to tell them to smile.

TIME AND SPACE SHIFTS.

Scene Ten

LEONIE, TAMARA, CLEO *are mid-recording. The recording light is on.* JESSICA*'s spot is still empty, it's been decorated and looks like a makeshift shrine, maybe they have added some fan mail to it.* IZZY *and* MILES *are in their usual places.* DARYL *watches on.*

CLEO. Put yourself in the shoes of a thirteen-year-old Tanzanian schoolgirl. Years of conflict. Turmoil. Upheaval. You're in a boarding school, run by white missionaries. An institution that wants to change you. Your best friend becomes the most precious person in your world. You finish each other's sentences. You tell each other bedtime stories. You hold hands when you're scared. Then your friend gets this horrible laughing plague. Surely that connection, that deep empathy is how it spreads between them.

LEONIE. Actually, Miles, you had a really good theory on empathy.

MILES. Cameo! Okay. So, if there was an empathy scale of like one to ten, Jessica would *definitely* be an eleven. By caring so much, and obsessing so much about Susan and the other victims at Slackerz, maybe her brain like tricked her into getting the silence.

CLEO. And since the water tests have come back totally inconclusive.

LEONIE. As did the handsyness.

CLEO. We've got to start looking to the past for answers and, empathy, sisterhood, this is powerful stuff you know.

LEONIE. Maybe that's how it spread at Slackerz in the first place?

TAMARA. Based on that logic then why don't we have it through of our empathy for Jess?

MILES. Because you all like talking too much, innit?

They laugh.

TAMARA. Someone cut his mic.

CLEO. No, seriously though, I think we might be onto something here.

TAMARA. Female empathy, really? Isn't it a bit like women are emotional and hysterical territory?

CLEO. Actually I think I can feel a story spill coming on…

TAMARA. Deep breath. And one two three. Spill.

CLEO. My mum passed away when I was thirteen and at her funeral, I wore this beautiful fuchsia dress she'd bought me, even though it was way too small for me by then. Anyway, everyone was crying but I felt… nothing? Dry eyes, like a desert. In the church, when my dad got up to give his eulogy, I suddenly got the giggles. And I couldn't stop. As everyone turns to look at me, horrified, my sister who is standing right beside me starts laughing, too. And we're stood there, holding hands, looking ridiculous in these too-tight dresses, in hysterics at our mum's funeral. Maybe it was a response to trauma, and empathy. Maybe that's what was going on with the girls in Tanzania, maybe that's why –

The recording light goes off and DARYL *interrupts the podcasters.*

DARYL. I'm so sorry, can we cut for a second?

CLEO. This guy.

DARYL. That was beautiful, Cleo. I really hate to be that guy but I wonder if actually Tanzania isn't the most gripping choice.

CLEO. Excuse me?

IZZY. I can do more research if that's what we need?

CLEO. Sorry, Izzy, hold on. I don't understand what's the problem?

DARYL. Well, it was an idea from Adam, actually, who has been doing his own research, I know, what a legend, and there was a more *local* case that he came across, what was it, Alex?

ALEX. A fainting epidemic at a Blackburn comprehensive in 1987, it mainly affected girls from the Irish Catholic community.

CLEO. Is this a joke?

DARYL. So Adam is a guru of listener engagement, but of course you know take it, leave it, this is your show, your choice. I'm always pro-choice.

CLEO. We'll definitely leave it, I think. Thanks, Daryl.

DARYL. Well, he's actually he is sort of insisting. We're trying hard to engage our core subscriber list, and well they'll be all over Blackburn –

CLEO. And exactly why do you think Blackburn will be more engaging than Tanzania?

DARYL. Maybe we could find a compromise and do both? Split the remaining time between them?

TAMARA. So why don't we keep going with Tanzania and then we can do a bit on the –

ALEX. Fainting epidemic in Blackburn in 1987.

TAMARA. Thanks, Alex. And then we can edit it in after?

DARYL. That's fantastic. Perfect. Thank you so much, girls. You really are the best.

It's tense for a moment. Everyone gets back into position. The recording light goes back on.

CLEO. So what I was trying to say is that in the early sixties the country had just emerged from decade upon decade of colonial rule and imperial oppression.

The NOTETAKER *fills up their glass with water from a jug on the table, it's quite noisy and disruptive.* CLEO *tries to ignore it, but it's clearly getting to her.*

And I think these young girls, in a missionary-run, you know, imperialist boarding school, were suddenly in a brand new, post-independent world and the stress and pressure of expectation.

The NOTETAKER *starts to very carefully open a foil-wrapped snack.*

Okay, sorry, can we stop? I'm so sorry, It's just the noise.

They all look at the NOTETAKER.

NOTETAKER. Who me?

CLEO. Yeah, like, maybe save your snack for later?

NOTETAKER. I had to skip lunch. I'm really hungry.

CLEO. Well it's just we're trying to record here and your snacking noises are really distracting.

NOTETAKER. Okay. Sorry?

The NOTETAKER *puts their snack away.*

CLEO. Sorry. Where was I?

IZZY. Tanzania. Post-independence.

CLEO. Right. Yeah, I can't do this any more –

CLEO *exits.*

TIME AND SPACE GLITCHES AND SHIFTS.

Scene Eleven

Tanzania, 1962. SUSAN *and* CHRISTINA *are listening to the radio, which has been playing the 'Advice to Tanzanian Mothers' public broadcast.* SUSAN *leans over and turns it off.*

CHRISTINA. Why won't you look at me?

SUSAN. I told you. I can't.

CHRISTINA. Why?

SUSAN. You know who the stupidest and saddest people in the world are?

CHRISTINA. Old people?

SUSAN. No. Our mums and our aunties. They're the saddest and stupidest people. Ever.

CHRISTINA. My mum's not sad.

SUSAN. Even the radio tells them what to do. An object is more powerful than them. That's sad. They're losers. Our mums are losers.

CHRISTINA. But they have to do what they're told. They're mums.

SUSAN. Exactly. But we don't.

CHRISTINA. Says who?

SUSAN. When I grow up I'm gonna be famous, and I'm gonna wear what I want, eat what I want, do what I want and have men, workers, cooking and cleaning and feeding me and no one will tell me what to do. Ever.

CHRISTINA. Why won't you look at me?

SUSAN. Because my dad told me not to.

CHRISTINA. Why not?

SUSAN. He said I have to avoid anything mildly entertaining.

CHRISTINA. We can't not ever look at each other again.

SUSAN. He said it's the only way to control the laughing. I don't want to make you laugh.

CHRISTINA. Why would you make me laugh. You aren't even funny.

SUSAN. It's not me. It's because you have a funny face.

She giggles. They hold their breath. It passes.

CHRISTINA. Do I really have a funny face?

SUSAN. No, you're pretty.

CHRISTINA. Eric doesn't think it's pretty. He said I look like a walrus and that means he thinks I'm ugly, because walruses are disgusting.

SUSAN. He's an idiot.

CHRISTINA. No, he's not. Don't be jealous.

SUSAN. In English class he asked me how to spell orange.

They laugh. They hold their breath. It passes.

CHRISTINA. Do you think we're possessed? Because Glory said she saw the devil in the mirror of the first-floor toilets and I swear I saw Martha's eyes flash red during Maths.

SUSAN. Maybe I don't believe in God.

CHRISTINA. Maybe you're possessed because you don't believe in him? So he's punishing you?

SUSAN. That doesn't make any sense.

CHRISTINA. Your face doesn't make any sense.

They giggle. They hold their breath. It passes.

Do you think Eric will ever ask me to be his girlfriend?

SUSAN. Do you think Eric's balls will ever drop? Because he sounds like a baby.

They giggle. They hold their breath. It passes.

CHRISTINA. If it's not the devil, or God, then what is it?

SUSAN. I don't know. Sometimes I think maybe, it's because the world... doesn't like us.

They are quiet.

I'm sorry I gave it to you.

CHRISTINA. You didn't give it to me.

SUSAN. I did.

CHRISTINA. No you didn't, okay?

SUSAN. Why are you so sure?

CHRISTINA. I just know, alright.

SUSAN. How do you know?

CHRISTINA *is silent*.

Tell me or I'll tell Eric you like him.

CHRISTINA. Fine. But don't get mad, yeah?

SUSAN. What is it?

CHRISTINA. I pretended. I was pretending that I got it too. I lied. I'm a liar and now I'm being punished for it.

SUSAN. Why would you do that?

CHRISTINA. I didn't want you to be alone. But now I'm not pretending any more and I'm scared.

SUSAN. I'm not scared. I'm just tired.

CHRISTINA. Of what?

SUSAN. Of living in a world that's not mine.

They are quiet for a second.

Let's practise for choir.

CHRISTINA. Do we have to?

SUSAN. My dad said if we don't practise every day we could lose our voices. Forever.

They giggle. They forget to hold their breath. They hold hands. They sing 'Good Times' by The Persuasions in perfect harmony.

TIME AND SPACE GLITCHES AND SHIFTS.

Scene Twelve

LEONIE *and* TAMARA *are in the studio.* CLEO, JESSICA *and* IZZY*'s chairs are all empty.* MILES *sits with the two podcasters,* ALEX *is on her iPad. The mood is tense. The podcasters are shaken.*

MILES. Cleo AND Izzy have it?

LEONIE. Looks like it.

MILES. I'm getting a bit scared now.

TAMARA. Me too.

ALEX. I should sort more fruit baskets. How do they feel about cantaloupe?

LEONIE. I don't know what that is.

ALEX *exits*. DARYL *enters*.

DARYL. Okay, gang, who wants to hear the good news?

LEONIE. What?

DARYL. So the silver lining to all this, is that people are *hooked*. Our audience share is up twenty per cent since Cleo and Izzy, you know. (*He mimes silence.*)

LEONIE. That's the good news?

DARYL. Well. The real news is. I've only gone and bagged you a live show! No one gets a live show first season at Trilogy. That's like season three level. This is HUGE.

TAMARA. How are we supposed to do a live show with only the two of us left?

DARYL. So that is an issue, and without Cleo's you know, energy, her storytelling, we're in danger of being a bit flat.

TAMARA. So we shouldn't do it. I'm worried about how we're going to get through the next episode let alone a live show?

DARYL. Well, Adam and I have been talking and we had a bit of a lightbulb moment, now it's a bit left field.

ALEX *enters*.

DARYL. We think Miles, could fill in as host for a little while –

MILES. Me? I don't know about this, man –

DARYL. Hear me out. You're all comfortable with Miles which is super-important to us… he already does his little cameos so the audience know him… and Adam really rates him. And he'd really just be filling the gap until this all blows over.

There is a pause, MILES *looks uncomfortable.*

So, what do you think, Miles?

MILES. This is a hundred per cent not my call.

TAMARA. We love Miles, obviously, but this is an all female podcast so that's slightly an issue.

MILES. I agree.

DARYL. You know, Adam's instinct for these things is pretty much always right. And Miles is great, right? We can all agree on that.

TAMARA. Miles is amazing, but putting someone who's a man in a show about elevating female voices, doesn't feel right.

LEONIE. And I don't think Cleo would approve.

TAMARA. Or Jessica.

DARYL. Well they're not here right now, so –

LEONIE. Can't we postpone the live show for a couple of weeks until we recruit a female host to step in?

DARYL. That could take months.

ALEX. Actually, I know someone who would be perfect, she's already a Trilogy host and loves –

DARYL. Do you know what I'm actually feeling really dehydrated. Could you fetch us some sparkling water, Alex. Thanks so much.

ALEX. Sure. I can do that.

ALEX *contains herself and exits.*

DARYL. Okay I'm going to level with you for a minute. There is a strong chance we won't get a second season.

LEONIE. What? You just said our listening rates were incredible.

DARYL. With Jessica, Cleo, and now Izzy going silent it's not just Slackerz that's under the spotlight now.

TAMARA. And Adam's response to that is to cancel our show?

DARYL. The live show is our chance to set the record straight about Trilogy, show that you guys love it here and also prove to Adam that this show is awesome.

LEONIE. He should know that already –

DARYL. Look, forget the podcast for a second, bigger picture, don't you want to get to the bottom of this outbreak? The live show will give Jess, Cleo, Iggy, Susan, and all the afflicted women the exposure their plight deserves, they need this.

The podcasters think it over.

LEONIE. Miles is basically an honorary Empowercaster I guess, right Miles?

MILES. I mean, I'd love to do it, but it's your call, a hundred per cent your call.

TAMARA. And this would only be for the next episode and the live show right?

DARYL. Exactly.

TAMARA *and* LEONIE *exchange looks, attempting to make a decision.*

Look, guys. Everyone is rooting for you. But at the end of the day, we've got to make a success out of the live show. And with Miles now in the mix Adam really thinks this it could work.

LEONIE. Sure, let's do this, Miles.

TAMARA. Okay. Yeah. Great.

DARYL. Fantastic!

MILES. I actually came across this crazy outbreak of compulsive twitching that spread like wildfire through a group of teenage cheerleaders in America – we should totally cover it in the next episode.

DARYL. That's genius, Miles!

TIME AND SPACE GLITCHES AND SHIFTS.

Scene Thirteen

Le Roy, 2011. It's the high-school prom. It looks and feels a bit like an American movie. Everyone is dancing in perfect unison to a song by Britney Spears, or Beyoncé, or another American pop star.

SUSAN *stands among them. She is still.*

Maybe we see images of beautiful women, of lips, of eyes, of legs, from magazines, from social media, from adverts, the way young girls wished they looked.

The dancing and the images build in tempo.

TIME AND SPACE GLITCHES.

Maybe a boy whispers into a girl's ear over the sound of the music. She listens and listens and then rolls her eyes. Perhaps a girl's skirt is lifted up by some boys as a joke.

TIME AND SPACE GLITCHES.

They twitch individually and then in unison.

TIME AND SPACE GLITCHES.

SUSAN *is twitching alone and everyone else is still. They all turn to look at her.*

CHRISTINA *also starts twitching with* SUSAN *and they stand centre stage.*

TIME AND SPACE SHIFTS.

A chorus of teenagers builds, some twitch and some don't, but all of their voices build into a frenzy. They speak to the internet, anonymously, their fears and anxieties melt into cyberspace.

FRANK. I started a rumour that the twitch bitches are devil worshippers.

CHRISTINA. I think the twitching might be a sexually transmitted disease.

MORGAN. I thought my life couldn't get any worse.

KAYLA. And now I'm a fucking twitch bitch. Yes, that's what they call us.

They twitch.

COURTNEY. The dumb doctor said I should see a shrink, but what if everyone thinks I'm crazy?

They twitch.

FRANK. My mum says that the girls who are twitching are attention-seekers.

RYDER. She says none of them are virgins. And she's right.

JORDAN. All my best friends are twitching except me, and now it's as if I'm the freak.

CLARA. Would it be really weird if I pretended to get it?

They twitch.

SUSAN. The school counsellor told me the twitching might be because of repressed guilt.

They twitch.

ERIC. My girlfriend got the twitch after she sucked my dick – is my cum poisoned? Or magic?

They twitch.

FRANK. Sometimes I think the rumour I started is true. I've seen their eyes when they twitch. They glow orange.

They twitch.

KAYLA. I eat dog biscuits because they are low in calories.

They twitch.

MORGAN. If I twitch myself to death, is it technically suicide?

They twitch.

CHRISTINA. God, it's me Christina. Can you hear me?

They twitch.

Please make it stop!

TIME AND SPACE GLITCHES AND SHIFTS.

Scene Fourteen

*In the wings on 'The Pulse', Trilogy's live event-space. The
audience murmurs in the background, there is commotion
backstage as* TRILOGY CREW *make final preparations, sound
checks, sorting mics, etc.* LEONIE *and* TAMARA *are about
to go on stage. They are wearing slightly garish 'Empowercast
LIVE' T-shirts, they are too big for them.*

LEONIE. This is exciting.

> TAMARA *doesn't respond.*

Are you okay?

TAMARA. Are you?

LEONIE. I think so, yeah.

TAMARA. It doesn't feel right doing this without the girls.

LEONIE. We're gonna smash it and when they're better, there'll
be a second season waiting for them and –

TAMARA. Can you just stop thinking about the podcast for one
second?

> TAMARA *spots* DARYL *laying out books on the set and
goes to investigate.* ALEX *enters.*

ALEX. Hey. I need to mic you up.

> ALEX *gestures for* LEONIE *to come over.* LEONIE
hesitantly stands up and goes over to ALEX *to have her mic
fitted.* TAMARA *is out of earshot.*

Excited?

LEONIE. Yeah. Bit nervous, this is a really big opportunity for
us.

ALEX. Yeah, sure it is.

LEONIE. Is Adam here yet?

ALEX. Adam's not coming.

LEONIE. Why not?

ALEX. He was never coming.

LEONIE. What?

ALEX. He's on a silent yoga retreat in Bali. It's been in the diary for months.

LEONIE. Oh, I thought Daryl said he'd be here.

ALEX. He only cares about the ratings so make sure you do a good job out there and the rest will take care of itself.

LEONIE. Sure, but we must be doing a pretty good job already if they've given us a live show in our first season.

ALEX. How can you not see what this is all about? They've only given you this show because they're hoping one of you goes silent live on air.

LEONIE. Sorry, what?

ALEX. This is all about ratings and spectacle. Surely, you've realised that by now. I thought you were smart.

LEONIE. Spectacle?

ALEX. They've been taking bets on you and Tamara. Daryl reckons you'll be the first to go.

LEONIE. Right, well there's no way I'm going out there now.

ALEX. What good would that do?

LEONIE. I don't have to do anything I don't want to do.

ALEX. Fine, don't then. Trilogy owns Empowercast anyway.

LEONIE....

ALEX. How did you not know that?

LEONIE. I'm not going out there.

ALEX. What about the women? I thought you really cared about getting to the bottom of this silence thing? Raising awareness. Being their voice. Don't you want to help them?

TIME AND SPACE SHIFTS.

Scene Fifteen

2011, New York City. SUSAN *and* CHRISTINA *are waiting backstage, in a green room, to go on the* Dr Derek Show. SUSAN *is no longer twitching, but* CHRISTINA *is still afflicted and twitches throughout the scene. The* CREW *for the* Dr Derek Show *begin to merge with* TRILOGY STAFF, *as they get the set ready.*

CHRISTINA. I don't want to go on TV like this. The whole world is gonna laugh at me.

SUSAN. But we have to let the world know what's happening so that –

CHRISTINA. I have an idea. Why don't you pray over me?

SUSAN. We've already tried that, like a hundred times.

CHRISTINA. Yeah but like try a different prayer.

SUSAN. What, like the Lord's Prayer?

CHRISTINA. No, like one from, like, your heart, like some deep shit, freestyle, maybe if you speak from your soul, he'll actually listen.

SUSAN. Alright. Okay. Dear Lord…

    SUSAN *can't bring herself to freestyle.*

CHRISTINA. Come on please. Put your hands over me. Like this.

SUSAN. Okay. Here it goes.

    SUSAN *recites several lines from 'Like a Prayer' by Madonna.*

CHRISTINA. That was beautiful. You should like take up poetry.

SUSAN. Thanks.

    They pause to see if it's worked. It hasn't.

CHRISTINA. Shit. It didn't work.

SUSAN. I'm sorry.

CHRISTINA. Okay. I know. Tie my arms down for, like, ten minutes.

SUSAN. We tried that last week. We have to go on in, like, any minute.

CHRISTINA. Don't be a bitch. Just because you're all better and I'm not.

SUSAN. I'm sorry.

CHRISTINA. It's not fair. How come you stopped twitching and not me? I don't understand. Is God still mad at me? What have I done wrong? I just wish someone would tell me, so I could repent.

CHRISTINA holds back her tears. The twitching gets worse.

SUSAN. Hey, it's alright.

CHRISTINA. It's not alright. I can't go on the *Dr Derek Show* like this. I'm a fucking freak.

SUSAN. Hey, why don't I put on some music. We can dance. That always helps right?

Their favourite song plays. Maybe they listen on an iPod and headphones. They dance, but CHRISTINA *keeps twitching. Eventually* SUSAN *goes over to her and holds her. They hold each other and move to the music, in an embrace.* CHRISTINA's *twitching eventually eases.*

CHRISTINA. Eric's gonna be watching. I don't want him to see me like this.

SUSAN. You know what? I think I get it. I think I get why this is happening to us.

CHRISTINA. You do?

SUSAN. Can't you see?

CHRISTINA. See what?

SUSAN. It's not us.
It's everyone else.

*TIME AND SPACE GLITCHES AS THE PAST AND
PRESENT MOVE CLOSER TOGETHER.*

Scene Sixteen

SUSAN *and* CHRISTINA *enter the Dr Derek Studio and take
their seats, as* TAMARA *and* LEONIE *also take their seats at
the Empowercast live show.*

TIME AND SPACE MOVE EVEN CLOSER TOGETHER.

MILES *and* PAUL *take their seats.*

CLARA *and* MORGAN *join* SUSAN *and* CHRISTINA. *They
all sit huddled together on a sofa, that is too small to hold them
all. They all twitch on and off, apart from* SUSAN.

*On both sets, crew and staff rush around, making last minute
adjustments, fixing make-up, etc.*

DARYL *rushes around, he's wearing a T-shirt that says 'The
Future is Female'.*

DR DEREK *is having a last minute make-up re-touch and being
briefed by the* PRODUCER.

His guests DR BUSHMAN *and* MR BARKER *take their seats.*

TIME AND SPACE MOVE EVEN CLOSER TOGETHER.

DARYL. So, everyone, this is Paul, he is doing a PhD on Mass
Hysteria .

DR DEREK. Hi girls. You look great. Don't they look just great,
Amy?

DARYL. It's great to have you here, Paul.

PRODUCER. You excited, girls?

PAUL. This is so exciting. This outbreak is groundbreaking.

CHRISTINA. I'm super nervous.

DR DEREK. You'll be fine. Just answer my questions and be yourselves.

DARYL *hands a piece paper to* LEONIE *and* TAMARA.

DARYL. Okay so here's the running order of stuff.

LEONIE. I thought I was doing the intro?

PRODUCER. Twenty seconds.

ALEX. We're going live in less that a minute.

DARYL. Adam thought it would be better if, as producer, I kicked things off.

TAMARA. Is Adam here?

PRODUCER. Fifteen seconds.

LEONIE. We agreed I'd do it.

ALEX. Ten seconds.

DR DEREK *stands in position*.

PRODUCER. Five seconds.

DARYL. Can we talk about it later?

DR DEREK. Here we go.

The CHEERLEADERS *twitch*.

Oh, and girls? Don't forget to smile.

They try their best to smile.

The crowd gets louder. The lights go up on the audience in the theatre, who become the audience in both studios. A theme tune plays.

TIME AND SPACE CRASH INTO EACH OTHER.

TIME AND SPACE UNITE.

The dialogue overlaps at points, it's fast and becomes more and more chaotic. Words in bold are said simultaneously in both worlds, by different characters. It feels like a fever dream.

DR DEREK. Welcome to the *Dr Derek Show.*

DARYL. What's up Empowercasters?

DR DEREK. What a show we have for you **today.**

DARYL. **Today** we are live in the studio with Leonie, Tamara, your boy Miles and our special guest Paul.

DR DEREK. We'll be diving deep into a mysterious outbreak of twitching at a suburban high school and asking our experts – What in the hell is going on?

MR BARKER. There's a litany of environmental horrors in the town of Le Roy, I don't know where to begin.

DR BUSHMAN. But the tests are all negative what do you say to that, Tim?

MR BARKER. Look, you've got a botched toxic waste clean-up of an unidentified brown substance literally oozing from the playing fields.

PAUL. I'm not saying women are more prone to this because they're emotionally unstable, I'm just saying that the literature on this doesn't lie.

DR BUSHMAN. By your logic then the whole student body and the faculty should be / afflicted too **surely**.

PAUL. And **surely**, we have to ask the question, why are women more prone to mass hysteria?

TAMARA. It's not called hysteria though.

LEONIE. It's Mass Psychogenic Illness.

MR BARKER. Well only time will tell / only time will tell, Dr Bushman.

DR BUSHMAN. But it's limited to these twenty or so students, and female students too, may I add.

MR BARKER. It's an environmental cover-up at a federal level, it goes all the way up and here you are saying it's because they're girls.

PAUL. A hundred per cent, the word hysteria is awful, I'm sorry, but the fact is that gender is key here is undeniable.

TAMARA. Rather than focus on gender can we –

PAUL. **Listen**.

DR BUSHMAN. **Listen** I am a professional medical doctor what are your qualifications?

PAUL. Listen. let me explain. It's the way women are sort of programmed to be empathetic, more emotional.

MR BARKER. I'm an environmental scientist actually and we're lucky it's only twitching, that school is so toxic that if you looked under their skirts, I wouldn't be surprised if you found a tail growing there.

DR DEREK. Okay, gentleman. That's quite enough.

MR BARKER. I'm **sorry**.

TAMARA. **Sorry**, Paul, but I hadn't finished speaking. The real question isn't what's wrong with women, but rather what in our world, in our politics, in our institutions, is at the –

PAUL. Sorry, if I could just say something?

DR DEREK. Dr Bushman, you've been working closely on this, what the hell is this thing and should we lock up our daughters?

PAUL. There's a real story in the numbers here, ninety-seven per cent of outbreaks of mass hysteria are predominately female, ninety-seven per cent.

LEONIE. It's not hysteria, stop saying **hysteria**.

DR BUSHMAN. This **hysteria** is a potentially a reaction to acute stress.

MR BARKER. Here we go suddenly the whole world has anxiety disorders. Our children are being poisoned.

MILES. You talk about the way woman have been programmed, like do you have an example?

PAUL. Of course. My book – *Hysterical* by Dr Paul Jenkins – focuses on this case study of fainting in Blackburn back in 1987, and turns out these girls were being abused –

DR BUSHMAN. I believe this is a psychological reaction to some sort of acute stress, or trauma.

DR DEREK. That sounds reasonable enough, but how the hell does it **spread from girl to girl**.

MILES. But how does it **spread from girl to girl**?

DR BUSHMAN. Well I'm afraid we just don't know. There isn't much research in this area.

PAUL. Look don't get me wrong I'm not suggesting that they're the weaker sex, they are just more susceptible to psychosomatic –

MILES. So you're saying they're faking it.

MR BARKER. So you're saying you don't know what you're talking about.

LEONIE *tries to speak, but* PAUL *speaks over her.*

PAUL. **You're putting words in my mouth**.

DR BUSHMAN. **You're putting words in my mouth**.

PAUL. Women are also socialised to cope with stress differently than men, they're more likely to talk to each other about their symptoms, which can spread outbreaks.

MILES. So now you're saying they're chatty.

PAUL. Come on give me a break, man.

DR DEREK. Hello, girls. We're all sitting wondering what the hell this thing is. What do you think?

CLARA. I don't know.

MILES. Sorry I don't mean to grill you, I just feel like it's not enough to put it down to so-called female qualities, it's a bit sexist.

PAUL. Come on.

DR DEREK. Well how did it all start? Why don't you tell us that?

LEONIE. Can I bring it back to –

When MILES *interrupts* LEONIE, *he might raise a hand without thinking, the way you do when you want someone to let you speak in a heated conversation. It infuriates* LEONIE.

MILES. One second. Just because you're qualified doesn't necessarily mean everything you say is fact.

MORGAN. Christina got it after homecoming dance and that's how it started.

DR DEREK. Well that leads us all to wonder, what the hell happened at this dance, Christina?

CHRISTINA. It was super-fun.

DR DEREK. Any drinking?

MORGAN. We're sixteen.

PAUL. I actually had this same conversation with your producer Daryl and Adam, just last night at the pub –

LEONIE. Oh you've met Adam have you?

PAUL. Yeah. We were at Cambridge together.

LEONIE. Had a little drink together? That's nice.

PAUL. Isn't he great? Such a visionary.

DR DEREK. Why do you think this is happening to you, Christina?

CHRISTINA. **I don't know**.

LEONIE. **I don't know**. We've never met him actually have we, Tamara?

PAUL. Oh, that's a shame.

LEONIE. Why are you actually here, Paul?

DEREK. Is there something you're not telling us?

PAUL. Have you even read the book?

CHRISTINA. **No**.

LEONIE. **No**.

PAUL. If you had actually read the book you'd see –

DR DEREK. What happened at the dance? You can tell me.

CHRISTINA. Nothing happened.

SUSAN. Leave her alone!

LEONIE. We only found out you were coming five minutes.
    ago –

PAUL. When I'm doing promo usually the hosts have actually
    prepared –

MILES. I do love the cover, man.

LEONIE. Miles!

DR DEREK. You said you were wearing a fuchsia dress? That's
    a nice colour.

TAMARA. We've done loads of research around this subject
    and we actually have lived experiences of everything you're
    talking about.

PAUL. Well, actually, many of my colleagues are female.

CHRISTINA. Yeah, my mom picked it out.

PAUL. And also if you look at some of my reviews, like
    'Absolutely excellent' – Dr Sam Jones.

DR DEREK. How short was your dress?

CHRISTINA. I don't know, like, normal length.

SUSAN. Why don't you just leave her alone?

SUSAN *gets up and her and the other* CHEERLEADERS *start smashing up the set of the* Dr Derek Show, *then of the* Trilogy *show, then everything else, by the end, there's almost nothing left.*

PAUL. You'll be surprised to hear that she is a woman. And she's lovely.

DR DEREK. Was it tight?

CHRISTINA. I don't know. I didn't do anything wrong.

DR DEREK. We are just trying to help you.

They smash.

LEONIE. Oh Sam JONES likes it?!

DR DEREK. Did you kiss any boys?

SUSAN. Stop being such a pervert.

PAUL. Are you feeling okay?

LEONIE. I'm great! I'm just finding it hard to talk about your fucking book when I'm so distracted by the fact we've got two men hosting our podcast about female empowerment, and our friends are sick.

They smash.

DR BUSHMAN. Are you sexually active?

CLARA. She only does hand stuff.

DARYL *motions for* LEONIE *to go back to the book.*

LEONIE. Oh, you want me to go back to the book, Daryl? Sure! I'd love to. I love this book.

CHRISTINA. Have I done something wrong?

LEONIE. But I love the pages, so many words!

DR BUSHMAN. Was that traumatic for you?

CHRISTINA. I... can we stop please?

They smash.

DR DEREK. You should smile more you're so much prettier when you smile.

LEONIE. Love this page.

DR BUSHMAN. Do you feel pressure to dress up?

LEONIE. And this page!

DR DEREK. You don't need to get so emotional.

LEONIE. I love this graph!

DR DEREK. You just need to tell the truth.

DARYL enters. The smashing stops.

LEONIE. Oh look, here comes Daryl. Are you gonna tell us what to do and what to say and how to speak? Do you know what, Daryl, you can just fuck right off. I don't know maybe it's this place, maybe that's why we're all losing our fucking voices and our minds.

Someone mutes LEONIE*'s microphone.*

DARYL. Wow, that got a bit heated. We love to see it. Love a good debate here at Trilogy. So before we say goodbye, we thought as a way to show solidarity with those afflicted with the silence, we could collectively, as one, just hold a minute's silence. Alex?

ALEX *holds her iPad up displaying a 60-second countdown.*

The actors and the audience sit in silence. Long enough to feel uncomfortable. The silence ends. ALEX*'s iPad bleeps. A notification.*

ALEX. Newsflash. Susan is talking again.

TIME AND SPACE GLITCHES.

Scene Seventeen

LEONIE *is alone in what was the studio, she stands among the wreckage from the previous scene, but it's as if only the audience can see the damage. Only two solitary microphones and the recording light remain intact.* DARYL *enters.*

DARYL. Hey.

LEONIE. Hi.

DARYL. You alright?

LEONIE. Yeah, not bad.

DARYL. No Tamara?

LEONIE. Yeah she might be on her way. I'm not really sure.

There's an awkward pause.

DARYL. Look I just wanted to say that shows get cut. It happens all the time. I really want you to know that it's not personal.

LEONIE. Bad luck.

Another awkward pause. DARYL *is building up the courage to say something.*

I better get set up.

DARYL. Actually, I also came to tell you that it's super unfortunate but we've actually decided to pull the bonus episode too. I'm so sorry.

LEONIE. Oh no. Really?

DARYL. It's out of my hands I'm afraid. Hands tied. (*He mimes hands tied.*)

LEONIE. But I have a guest coming, she should be getting here any minute.

DARYL. I'm so sorry. I'll tell Alex to meet her at reception and explain. Don't worry, she'll sort it.

LEONIE. Okay. Well. That's a shame.

DARYL. I know. I know. I'm so sorry. Look I better go. Late for meeting. As always.

LEONIE. Okay. Well. See you later.

DARYL *walks away and then turns around at the door.*

DARYL. And Leonie?

LEONIE. Yeah?

DARYL. There's free kombucha in the atrium.

DARYL *exits.*

LEONIE *sits in silence. It goes on for a little longer than is comfortable.*

Eventually SUSAN *walks in.*

SUSAN. Hi Leonie? Reception sent me up here, am I in the right place?

LEONIE. Oh, hi.

SUSAN. I'm Susan.

LEONIE. Yeah, of course. Thanks so much for coming. Did reception not –

SUSAN. It's so nice to meet you finally. I feel like I already know you.

LEONIE. Yeah, you too.

SUSAN. Is it just us two?

LEONIE. Right yeah. Did they not tell you at reception?

SUSAN. Oh wow. This is so exciting. I've actually always wanted to be on a podcast. Can I sit down?

LEONIE. Yeah, of course.

SUSAN. I listen to podcasts all the time. And not just true crime ones. I have super eclectic taste. When I couldn't speak. You know I really started to listen. I'm a bit nervous actually. Sorry, am I talking too much? My mum said it's like I'm making up for all the lost time, I can't shut up these days.

LEONIE. So –

SUSAN. Do you speak into here?

LEONIE. Yeah, that's right.

SUSAN. Wow, it's so cool here. I thought there would be more people, like crew and stuff.

LEONIE. Actually Susan, I'm so sorry but –

SUSAN. Thank you for this by the way. To be able to tell my story, with my own voice, like literally, it's really important to me. I feel like everyone's been speaking for me and now I'm ready to speak for myself.

LEONIE. You don't need to thank me.

SUSAN. Are these for me?

LEONIE. Yeah.

SUSAN *puts the headphones on.*

SUSAN. Are you gonna switch that light on?

LEONIE. Which light?

SUSAN. The one that says recording.

LEONIE. Oh yeah. I think the bulb might be broken or something.

SUSAN. Oh okay. Do you need to fix it?

LEONIE. Actually Susan. The truth is –

The recording light suddenly goes on.

SUSAN. Oh look, it's working.

LEONIE *looks up and sees* ALEX *in the control room. Maybe* ALEX *smiles at her. It would be the first time we've seen her smile. Or maybe we don't see* ALEX *and the light just comes on by magic.*

LEONIE. Great. Okay. Right. Let's get started, then. So just be yourself. I'll ask some questions and you just tell your story. In your own words. Ready?

SUSAN. Yeah. Ready.

LEONIE. And one two three. Spill.

> SUSAN *takes a deep breath in.*
>
> *The world goes dark.*
>
> *End.*

ALMEIDA
THEATRE

ALMEIDA PARTICIPATION

Our Participation programme inspires and engages young people and our local community, giving them opportunities to create theatre with the most exciting artists working in the industry today. Those participating in our projects are in a two-way dialogue with us, learning from directors, actors, writers and producers, and also influencing and shaping our work in the future.

MORE INFORMATION

Twitter and Instagram @ATParticipate
almeida.co.uk/participate
020 7288 4916
participate@almeida.co.uk

Director of Participation and
Work for Young People   Dani Parr
Participation Producer   Simon Stephens
Participation Associate   Abi Falase
Schools Producer   Annys Whyatt
Participation Assistant   Montel Douglas
Participation Producer Assistant   Lauren Joyce-Smith

Almeida Participation is incredibly grateful to all the individuals, companies, trusts and foundations who support our work.

www.nickhernbooks.co.uk

facebook.com/nickhernbooks

twitter.com/nickhernbooks